Microsoft Teams Guide for Success:

Learn in a Guided Way to Exchange Messages, Documents, Participate in Videoconference and Virtual Meetings with Your Colleagues and Clients | Big Four Consulting Firms Method

Copyright © 2022
Kevin Pitch

TABLE OF CONTENTS

INTRODUCTION..3

1 MICROSOFT TEAMS COMPARISONS 11

2 SOFTWARE INTERFACE AND USE...14

3 TEAMS AND CHANNELS..18

4 COMMUNICATE VIA CHAT AND VIDEO CHAT OUTSIDE YOUR ORGANIZATION 25

5 THE BEST TEAMS APP...26

6 TIPS, TRICKS & FAQ WITH COMMON PROBLEMS AND SOLUTIONS....33

7 ADMINISTRATOR TEAMS 36

8 THE STRATEGIC SHORTCUTS 43

9 CONCLUSION..46

INTRODUCTION

Microsoft Teams launched in September 2016, offering organizations a chat-enabled collaboration service for medium to large teams. Microsoft Teams is designed to enable you to manage and provide easy access to conversations easily. With the integration of Office 365 Groups, Microsoft Teams can be an option for company-wide communications and collaboration on any number of channels, from a team chat room to a single-user channel. Learn how Microsoft Teams can enhance your productivity by giving employees the tools they need to communicate more easily and collaborate more efficiently.

Microsoft Teams is a proprietary business communication platform, belonging to the Microsoft 365 family of products. Its features include workspace chat, file storage, video conferencing, and application integration. While it can be confusing initially, the software has many advantages and is an excellent choice for most businesses.

1.1   What is Microsoft Teams?

Microsoft Teams is a collaboration and communications tool available as a stand-alone app or as part of a bundle. It offers several features, including chat, video conferencing, and file sharing. It also lets users create a shared background and avatar. In addition, Microsoft Teams includes reports and analytics that help users track usage statistics.

Microsoft Teams is part of Microsoft 365, which includes other productivity tools, like Outlook, and comes with security features. It costs $5 per user per month. It supports up to 10,000 participants. It also offers integrations with popular third-party apps like Trello, Asana, and Zoom.

Adoption is key to Microsoft Teams' success. Once a team has accepted the new features and processes, real results can be achieved. But it's crucial to remember that a company cannot expect all employees to switch overnight. Therefore, it's essential to consider any potential issues that might arise as the new software is adopted.

Teams features include built-in online meetings and audio/video conferencing. Meetings can last up to 60 minutes. Teams also offers unlimited storage for personal files. Users can also integrate Office apps with the service. Developers can also build custom apps for Teams. Microsoft has also partnered with hardware vendors to provide video conferencing hardware.

Microsoft Teams integrates with all of Microsoft's other apps and services. For example, you can create files right in Teams channels. You can also work with team SharePoint sites through Teams. In addition, Teams is tightly integrated with Microsoft Power Apps, which allows you to create and share low-code apps. The platform can also help you organize your conversations by letting you create and manage conversations in channels.

1.2 Basic algorithm work of Microsoft Teams

We refer to Microsoft Teams as a team collaboration platform offering a variety of features. These features are divided into different user groups. Each group has its purpose and has its preferences. Understanding how these user groups interact with the platform is crucial to creating a successful collaboration experience. Here are a few things you should know.

Microsoft Teams has two different network protocols, UDP and TCP. UDP has a higher MOS score and is less likely to have a high down count. Both protocols can be affected by low bandwidth. Therefore, choosing the proper network protocol for your specific needs is crucial.

1.3 Where can you buy it or download

Microsoft Teams is a collaborative messaging software you can use to communicate with other team members. The program is available for desktops and mobile devices and is compatible with most App Stores. A free trial is an excellent option if you're unsure whether you want to buy a license.

Microsoft Teams is a versatile messaging app that organizes tasks and initiates team conversations. It also offers features such as video conferencing and shared workspaces to help you collaborate with coworkers and clients from any location. You can also perform collaborative tasks like sharing files, hosting meetings, and setting up tasks in real-time.

You can download the Teams app from the Microsoft Store. It is available for Windows 10 and 11. Although you can download the Teams app from the Microsoft Store, it will not be included in the Office 365 bundle.

Microsoft Teams is a collaborative workspace for Windows computers. It syncs data across platforms so you can use it on a desktop, mobile, or tablet. It also integrates with Office 365 and OneNote to make it easier for you to work with others. So if you're considering using the program to improve your business, it's worth trying.

Microsoft Teams offers essential features, including video conferencing, file sharing, and chatting. It also has tools for sharing ideas, assigning tasks, and moving projects off a whiteboard. In addition, you can sync Microsoft Teams with your Exchange calendar, so it will automatically show up in Outlook.

1.4   How do we get MS Teams free?

It is possible to access the Teams interface minus subscribing to the Microsoft 365 plan. The only disadvantage is that the free version of the Microsoft Team is not packed with many of the benefits of the premium versions – but you will still get some basic features you can relate with. Intimate yourself with the steps below to get access to a free version of the Team interface;

-        Navigate to your favorite browsing apps (preferably Chromes) on your computer, and type https://www.microsoft.com/en-us/microsoft-teams/free.

-        Once the address has loaded, tap the **_sign up for free button_**

-        You will be prompted to enter your e-mail address. You can sign in with the Microsoft account you had previously created or even create a new account entirely. Verification will be required if you are utilizing Microsoft service for the first time. To verify your mail, enter the code sent to your mail into the box provided.

-        After the Account verification and you have successfully signed in to your Microsoft account, you either download Teams app using your PC or to start using it via the web.

- Tap the web-based option if you are interested in using the web-based version of Teams. On tapping, you will be taken to Teams web portal (https://teams.microsoft.com).

- The "how to invite people to Teams" page will be displayed next. Select "got it" and you then have access to Teams workspace. A congratulatory message will pop up, welcoming you into the Teams world.

1.5 Getting Teams through the Microsoft 365

Signing up to your preferred Microsoft 365 business plan automatically gets Microsoft Teams included. Users can still enjoy a free version of Microsoft 365 without using their money to subscribe, but it does not come with the Microsoft Team. Let us take a look at how you can get access for free.

- Navigate to your preferred web browser from your desktop, and visit https://www.office.com/.

- Tap the "Get office icon."

Figure 1: Welcome to Office

- Once you tap the "get office icon" you will be redirected to https://www.microsoft.com/en-us/microsoft-365/buy/compare-all-microsoft-365-products?tab=1&rtc=1, where you can compare between existing Microsoft plans. There are two tabs; ***Home plan and business plan***.

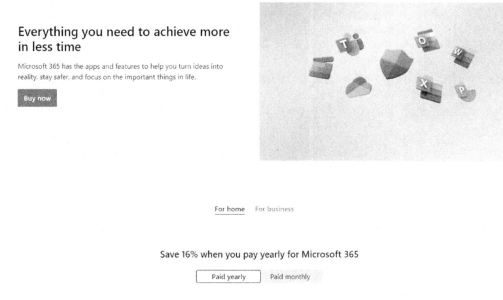

Everything you need to achieve more in less time

Microsoft 365 has the apps and features to help you turn ideas into reality, stay safer, and focus on the important things in life.

Buy now

For home   For business

Save 16% when you pay yearly for Microsoft 365

Paid yearly   Paid monthly

Figure 2: Find the right solution for you

- Select "***For business***" tab to get started and choose your plans.

- When you click the "***For business***" *tab,* you can choose between the four available plans. The business basic also features Microsoft Teams.

Reimagine productivity with Microsoft 365 and Microsoft Teams

Figure 3: For Business Packages

- Navigate the page to the bottom and select ***"Try free for one month"*** as an option of the Microsoft 365 business basic or any other plan that suits you.

- A page where you will be required to answer some basic questions and provide some information will be prompted.

- Provide each piece of information carefully, and the last step will get you set for your selected plan.

- Immediately after you provide all the information, your free trial will be ready, and you can tap on the *"Get started icon"* to continue.

1.6 Where can you use it?

You can use Microsoft Teams to collaborate with your coworkers. To start using it, you must sign in to the Microsoft account. To sign in, visit Microsoft's Teams website and click sign-in button. Select appropriate username and choose if you want to use Teams for business purposes. You must also agree to Terms of Service and Privacy Policy.

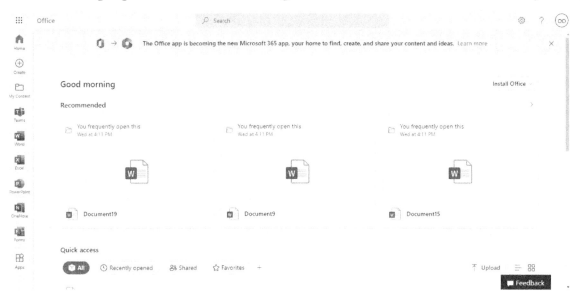

Figure 4: Office Online

Microsoft Teams also lets you invite people to join a meeting. You can send out invites to people using a shareable link, your e-mail contact list, or a direct e-mail. If you're using the web version, you'll need to allow permission for people to join the meeting. Once they're in, they'll receive notifications. They'll also be prompted to provide their camera and microphone access.

Microsoft Teams also lets you share documents and media with others. You can also screen share, whiteboard, or breakout into virtual rooms. It also supports enterprise security and compliance. The app also includes a default document library folder. If you're using the app for business purposes, you should set permissions to restrict access to sensitive information.

Microsoft Teams is integrated into Windows 365 and Azure Virtual Desktop. It has many business benefits and integrates with popular desktop and mobile devices. It is also compatible with many third-party meeting room devices. Microsoft has also integrated Teams with HoloLens, a headset that lets you see experts in real-time.

Microsoft Teams is a productivity application that integrates apps and tools in one place. It enables collaboration with others on projects and improves productivity and efficiency. The app also integrates information from Microsoft Outlook and SharePoint lists into the workspace. It also allows you to schedule meetings, video chats, and file sharing with colleagues and friends. The service is compatible with multiple operating systems, and you can install it on your computer, tablet, or mobile device.

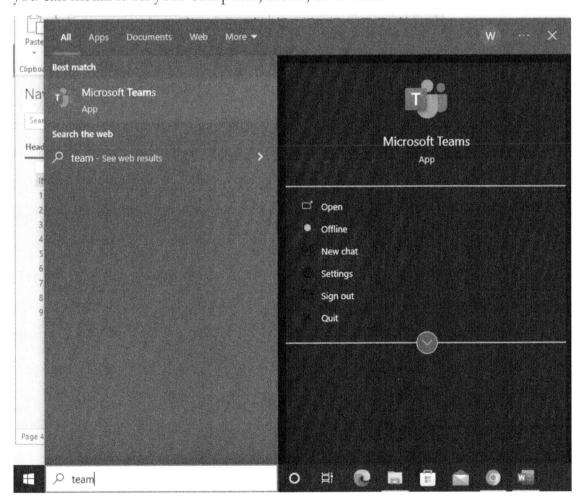

Figure 5: Accessing MS Teams

1.7 MS Teams extension and where to download them

Many useful extensions are available whether you're using MS Teams for teamwork or as an enterprise tool. Bonusly, for example, makes it easy to express appreciation to coworkers. With its easy-to-use interface, you can grant colleagues a bonus, review their performance, and see the latest achievements.

Another helpful extension is Tactiq, which lets you take screenshots during meetings and export transcripts. This extension connects with your Microsoft Teams account and displays the meeting transcript in real-time. You can also take notes on sentences in the meeting and save them later for future reference.

Microsoft Teams users can also use Polly, which allows them to create surveys using Microsoft Teams. Polly helps you to collect opinions from your team and votes on questions quickly and easily. To use this extension, add the question and answers you want to ask and mention the @polly in the chat.

2 MICROSOFT TEAMS COMPARISONS

You're probably curious about how these tools compare if you're comparing Microsoft Teams with Slack, Skype, or Google Meet. These comparisons will give you an idea of what you can expect from each application. But before you choose a platform, you should know that these products don't have the same features.

2.1 Microsoft Teams vs. Slack

Microsoft Teams is a chat-based workspace available in Office 365 and is an excellent choice for large organizations. It integrates Skype and other services and includes private group chats. Slack, however, focuses on bringing all team communication into one place. While Teams is more complex to setup, it does offer some advanced features that other messaging apps don't. For example, it allows users to change the font color and add bullet points to their messages.

Microsoft Teams and Slack offer many features that make them useful for large enterprises. For example, Slack offers video conferencing but can only support up to 25 users simultaneously. Unlike Slack, however, Microsoft Teams offers screen sharing on all plans, including free. In addition, Teams supports live events and captioning of videos. Teams and Slack are great options for small businesses, but the two have some differences. Microsoft Teams has more features and is cheaper. It also offers more options, including unlimited message history. Teams also allows teams to screen-share and can be more flexible for teams that don't use Microsoft 365.

Microsoft Teams is the market leader for collaboration. Both tools have a good user experience and advanced security and compliance features. Microsoft Teams is also GDPR and DLP-compliant.

2.2 Microsoft Teams vs. Skype

While Microsoft Teams is not a direct replacement for Skype for Business Online, it provides several features that make video chat and phone calls easier. In addition, teams bring together various tools such as chat, calls, file sharing, and third-party apps into one seamless experience. As a result, Teams meet the diverse communication needs of distributed workplaces.

Teams is a powerful communication tool that integrates with dozens of third-party apps. It is also customizable and can be used for collaboration. For instance, you can embed games and other applications into your workflow. However, Skype doesn't support such integrations. For business use, Teams has more business-oriented features.

Microsoft Teams is designed to foster collaboration. On the other hand, Skype for business was originally intended to be a communications platform. Collaboration features were added almost as an afterthought. Microsoft Teams enables meetings with up to 250 participants. It also has advanced video conferencing capabilities. Additionally, you can share your desktop, screen, and single applications with team members. You can also use advanced features such as transcription and translation.

Teams offers more features than Skype. It has a more intuitive interface and supports more collaboration. Teams also have a more robust search feature and bookmarks. It also supports Microsoft Cloud architecture, which ensures excellent security, zero downtime, and customizable data governance policies.

2.3 Microsoft Teams vs. Google Meet

One of the biggest differences between Microsoft Teams and Google Meet is that Teams runs in a Microsoft 365 environment. As a result, your team can collaborate on files, presentations, and other items. On the other hand, Google Meet lets you share your entire screen, browser tabs, and individual files. In addition, Google Meet is a browser-based service that is much easier to use than Microsoft Teams.

Another significant difference between Google Meet and Microsoft Teams is that Google Meet allows you to keep a live video feed on screen while presenting. In contrast, Microsoft Teams will enable you to disable it. Google Meet also lets you customize your background and connection quality. Despite the differences, each platform offers plenty of features to boost collaboration.

Google Meet has a more streamlined interface and fewer buttons. The two programs also share similar video-conferencing features. Google Meet also offers a variety of integrations, including integrations with Microsoft Office, Gmail, and Zapier. You can also dial into a meeting via phone.

Google Meet is free for small businesses and individuals, but it's also available to anyone with a Google account. It allows you to have 24-hour 1:1 calls and 1-hour-long group meetings with three or more users. You might want to consider Zoom if you're not a business user. Microsoft Teams is a better choice for large teams.

3 SOFTWARE INTERFACE AND USE

3.1 Screen sharing in Microsoft teams

Regular screen sharing involves showing presentations or participants via a process or tool. All partakers, except unconfirmed guests, are in a position to share the screen. Unconfirmed guests will be offered a number and should wait in the lobby until the organizer grants them access.

Begin sharing the screen

Screen sharing can happen in a conversation, meeting, or call.

- Click screen share icon during a call, meeting, or chat.
- You may choose to share:

The entire desktop

Only one screen/window

Whiteboard

A PowerPoint presentation

3.2 Scheduling a Meeting

Scheduling a meeting in Microsoft Teams is a straight forward process. To schedule a meeting:

1. First, you need to click on the purple "Schedule a Meeting" button.

2. Next, create a title for the meeting and enter all relevant information.

Note - If you don't specify the location of the meeting, it will be displayed as a Microsoft Teams meeting, so you may choose to leave the location field blank.

3. The next thing you want to do is invite your attendees, and to do this, enter their names into the "Invite People" section.

Note – You can find the scheduling assistant very useful here, as you can use it to see if the individual you're inviting is available for the meeting.

4. Finally, Click "Schedule."

5. You will see a pop-up with the details of the meeting you just scheduled. From the pop-up, you can join the meeting, cancel the meeting, and chat with participants (this will open a separate chat window). You can also edit the meeting information, close the window, and return to Microsoft Teams.

3.3 Joining a Meeting

Joining a Teams meeting is a straight forward process. You can decide to join the meeting via your Outlook calendar or your "Meeting" tab on Teams. If you are joining from the Outlook Calendar, just click on the link "Join Microsoft Teams meeting," or if enabled, dial the toll-free or local number and type in your given conference ID number when requested.

If you are joining the meeting directly from Teams, locate your "Meetings" tab, click on the meeting, and finally, click the "Join" tab at the top-right corner of your screen.

3.4 Share and control the screen

To share the screen with other participants in the first call, click Share screen button located towards the bottom and select the screen you want to display in the group. By doing this, other users will see and follow the screen without having to leave the video call.

Other users can control your screen if they get permission. You can let other participants control the screen by selecting their names in the bar at the top of the call.

3.5 User Availability (Status)

Before you call someone, it is possible to check if they are available, away, busy, or do not disturb mode. On the Calls tab, you notice a colored circle next to the profile picture of the person. The color is a representation of their current state.

If you call a member who cannot answer the call while busy, you may choose to notify them when their status comes to On. Remember that availability does not necessarily mean that they can call you. Other tasks may need their attention, though such an announcement can be a temporary guide to the best time to contact individuals.

- Click the person's icon/profile picture you wish to monitor on your status screen.

- A pop-up window will appear with more information about the contacts. Click on the chat icon. The private conversation opens.

- On the screen's left side, you will notice a list of used conversations. Right-click or click the ellipse button on the desired person's name.

- Click report when available. Whenever available, you will note a pop-up appearing on the screen.

Monitor their status

- You should right-click (or click the ellipse button) the person's name on the chat screen.

- Click Disable Notifications.

3.6 How to React to chat messages

It is possible to react to someone's message without responding. You may use an emoji like thumbs up, surprise emoji and more.

To do so, hover the mouse over the message or you may select the ellipsis against the message to see the reaction options. You then choose the appropriate reaction you desire. The more people react to a message with same emoji, the number of such reaction increases. Reactions can be significant in recognizing a message without typing out a reply.

Once you are comfortable with the Interface and the capabilities, using Teams and navigating around it is relatively straightforward.

- Toolbar- On the left side, we have the toolbar, which has a variety of functions. In addition, we have:

- *Activity*-It demonstrates every single item of your areas of interest as well as what you must be aware of that has taken place.

- *Chats*-It gives you the ability to send messages to your fellow contemporaries. You can select specific individuals or a number of them to start a conversation.

- *Teams*- You can construct channels here and check out the different groups you're a part of.

- *Meetings*- Here, you can launch a session and immediately continue to schedule a meeting.

- *Calls*-Here, you can easily make calls directly from your contact list.

- *Files*-You can share data and upload files to the 'OneDrive'cloud.

- *[...]*- The three dots enable you to add more functions from the toolbar. For example, you can extend Microsoft Teams depending on your requirements.

- *Apps*- here, you will obtain additional applications for your Teams.

- *Help*- Help provides more information about the operation of the Teams application.

- *The Channel Bar* -the channel bar provides you with more possibilities whenever you've chosen one of the tools for use. Additionally, it facilitates the organization of conversations when making use of the Meeting tool.

- Command/Search Box -the command box is at the very top of the application. You can use it to locate contacts and perform actions quickly at the beginning of an application when you input a slash "/."

- The Tabs-The tabs enable you to navigate between Team pages more efficiently. Additionally, you can add a tab using the + sign.

- The Conversation box -outlines your online interactions and talks with different individuals and organizations.

- Chatbox - using this will allow you to perform text-based communication within Teams.

4 TEAMS AND CHANNELS

Create a New Team

Follow the steps below when you need to create a new team.

- Open MS Teams software.

- Select Teams icon located to the left file tab.

- Click "Join or Create a Team" link. Consider the goals for the new team. Put in mind what the leaders for the new team intend to achieve, if you already had another team with similar goals. Are members same as those for the previous team or there are new ones?

Figure 6: Create a Team

Decide the kind of team to set up.

- Private: Members will seek permission to join the team.

- Public: Anyone can join this team. It is open to everyone.

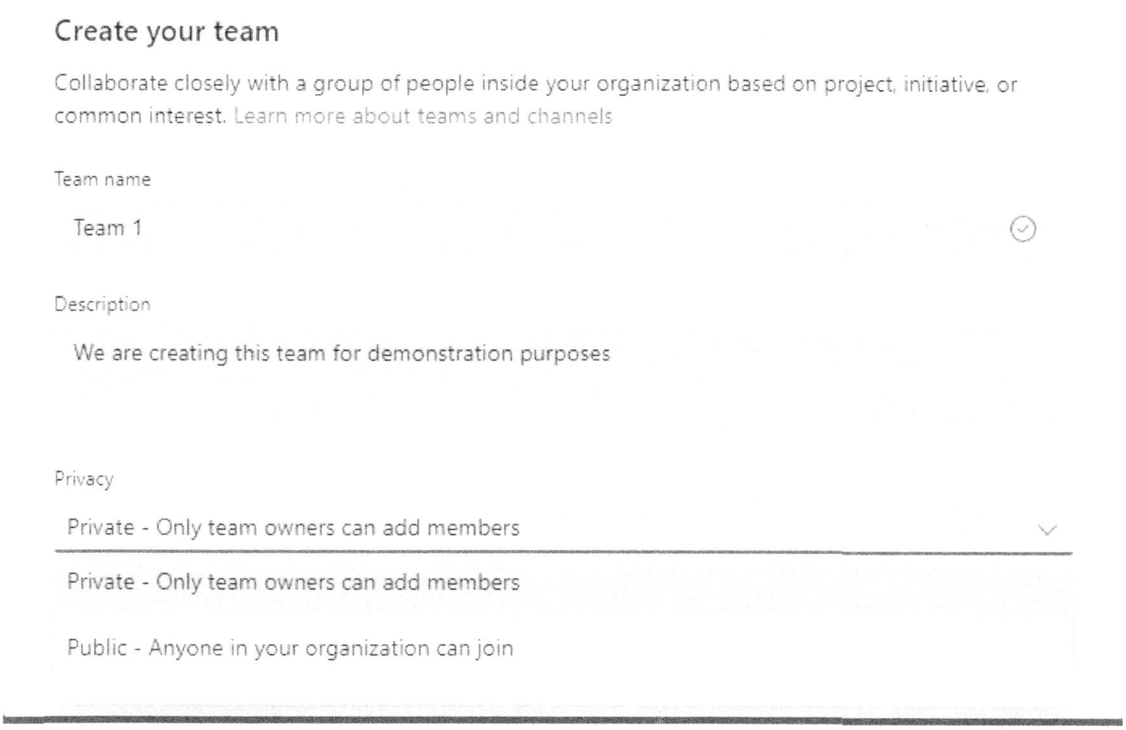

Create your team

Collaborate closely with a group of people inside your organization based on project, initiative, or common interest. Learn more about teams and channels

Team name

Team 1

Description

We are creating this team for demonstration purposes

Privacy

Private - Only team owners can add members

Private - Only team owners can add members

Public - Anyone in your organization can join

Figure 7: Creating your team

Type the name and summary of your new team, and then press Build. Teams will take a few moments to do their job by building a new team for you. Once done, your new team shows up in your list of teams to the left file tab. Note that when a new team is formed, a channel named General is created instantly.

4.1 How to Invite People to Your Team

- Create your new team.

- Choose the private or public privacy type of the group. You will get a dialogue box giving you an opportunity to welcome people to join once the team has been set up.

- In the search box, type the names of the people to add to your team. Your search feature immediately scans and populates a text box depending what you type. The results happens in real time as you type.

- Once the right person appears in the list, select the individual's name before selecting Add.

- Add as more members to the team as you wish.

Add members to Team 1

Start typing a name, distribution list, or mail enabled security group to add to your team.

Newton   Add

KN	Karisa **Newton** W1424214
KN	David **Newton** W1383379
JN	Jonathan **Newton** W1696174
KN	Krystal **Newton** W1281926
SN	Scott **Newton** W1838647

Skip

| TN | Taylor **Newton**
W1949873 |

Figure 8: Adding team members

All invited users will get a notification about their team membership.

Follow these steps when you wish to invite individuals to a public or private team once it is already created:

- To see a summary of your teams, click the Teams symbol in the left file tab.

- Tap the ellipse beside the team name you want to ask somebody to join. It will open a drop-down menu with some options.

- Choose Add Member from the drop-down menu that shows. Next, the Add Members dialogue box should appear.

- In the text box, simply type names of people you wish to add to the team.

- Once you find the right person, click the names of the people and Add. The users will be notified depending on how alerts have been set up.

4.2 Creating a New Channel

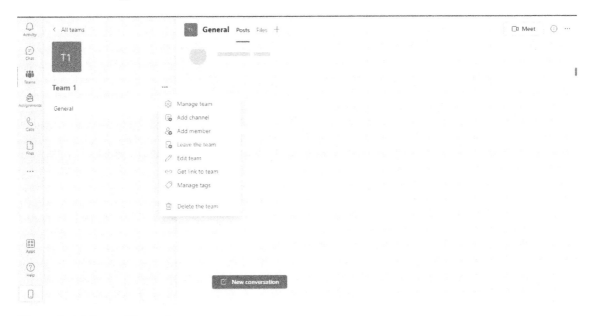

Figure 9: Adding a Channel

At the heart of a team are channels. Teamwork and communication happens inside channels. Channels sit inside a team; therefore, a team is made up of one or more channels. A channel acts as a single place where team members can share messages, files and tools.

- You can organize a channel depending the project, group or relevancy.

- It is possible to make changes on how they get the notifications from a channel.

- Threads are good for side conversations that focused & organized within given channels.

Every team begins with the default "**General**" channel. Such is there to discuss general topics related to the purpose of the team. You can have a wiki page as a general landing page for your team. For each other topic, i.e., project, task, etc. create a new channel.

The best approach is to bundle all related content in one place – under a channel. There is a limit of 200 channels per team – currently, including deleted channels.

4.3 Create a channel

1. You Click the **ellipses** icon for more options to the right of the team in question in the "**Teams**" pane.

2. You Click the "**Add channel**" option in the pop-out menu to create a channel.

3. You Enter text in the "**Channel name**", "**Description (optional)**" fields, Select from the "**Privacy**" drop-down field and check the "**Automatically show this channel in everyone's channel list**" tick box.

Lastly, you Click the "**Add**" button at the bottom to complete the channel creation on the "Create a channel for '[team name]' team" screen.

Note: *You can always "**Edit this channel**" and change the "Channel name" and the "Description" text box fields, and the "Automatically show this channel in everyone's channel list" tick box.*

*You cannot change the "**Privacy**" field after the channel has been created. You will need to create a new channel with new privacy settings.*

4. You will see your channel's landing page on the larger right pane of the TEAMS App window as illustrated below in Figure 42. The new channel also has the name of the team member who created it followed by the phrase "**[Full Name] set this channel to be automatically shown in the channels list**" from the Selection previously made when creating the team.

5. You Click the **ellipses** icon to the right of your channel and Select the "**Hide**" option from the pop-out menu to hide your team.

6. You Click the "**# hidden channel**" link (in the "Teams" pane) to view the hidden channel(s). This can easily be missed.

7. You Click the "**Show**" option to the right of the channel in question to show that channel.

Tip: *Once your channel has been hidden, the text formatting of that channel will change to italic text. When you Click away from your channel, it will be hidden under the link something like "**# hidden channel**".*

8. You Hold down the left mouse button and move the team in question up or down in the "**Teams**" pane. Figure 45 below illustrates the "**Communications**" team dragged from bottom to top of "**Your teams**".

Note: *When it comes to ordering your channels; you should practice naming your channels with a number prefix. Renaming a channel retrospectively however does not rename the SharePoint Online folder – you will have to rename the folder on your SharePoint site also.*

Tip: *You should create a channel only if it is required (as you would when you create a team). This means that you create a channel when there is a requirement for it or that you have use for it.*

9. You Create a Private channel as you would anyone channel, except for the "**Privacy**" drop-down field, you Select the "**Private – Accessible only to a specific group of people within the team**" option. You Click the "Add" button at the bottom to finish creating the private channel where the new channel will have a padlock icon to the right of that channel's name.

4.4 CALENDAR

The Calendar function is one of the many tools included in Microsoft Teams. These tools help in boosting productivity and improving communication amongst staff members. It is possible for team members to schedule meetings directly within the Microsoft Teams app, specify the meeting's details, and add other team members so that they are not only informed of the event but also have it added to their synced Microsoft Teams calendar. The shared calendar within Microsoft Teams facilitates this.

How the Microsoft Teams Calendars Function

Microsoft Teams is a collaboration tool that is designed for companies or groups, and as a result, it is organized with a group, or team, as its primary point of emphasis. You sign into MS Teams group using your email address, but in most cases you may not. You will use the enterprise email address provided for you to access Teams as well as any other Microsoft 365 apps or services relevant to you.

Additionally, the MS Teams app includes only one primary calendar shared among all the team members. Group affiliates may add events or meetings to this calendar. Such additions will immediately appear on other group members' calendars. If you expect a person to attend an event or forum on the calendar, you can add them to the event or meeting.

The Step-by-Step Guide to Creating an Event on the Shared Calendar for Microsoft Teams

In this section, we'll go through the steps to take when creating an event known as a meeting in MS Teams.

Please follow the instructions below to create a shared calendar event in Microsoft Teams.

1. Launch the Microsoft Teams software.
2. Click the Calendar option.
3. Select the "New meeting" option from the menu.
4. Use the drop-down option at the top of your page to select appropriate time zone for your location.

NOTE: You do not need to be concerned about your team members' different time zones because the start time of your meeting will automatically adjust depending on their time zones.

5. Give your meeting a name in the "Add title" section.
6. Put the names of the people whose attention you would like to draw to the upcoming event in the section labeled "Add required attendees."

You can share this calendar event with other individuals who are not members of your MS Teams group or who may not even use MS Teams at all by typing their complete email addresses in place of their name.

By selecting 'Optional,' you can add group members you wish to inform about the meeting but must not necessarily attend.

After setting up the meeting, each of the invited parties will receive an invitation at the email address associated with their account.

7. The next step is to determine when the meeting will begin and end.

8. If the meeting is to occur on a regular basis, proceed by clicking on the option that says "Does not repeat" to access the menu and select the options that best fit your needs to turn the meeting into a recurring event. Choose the "does not repeat" option if you don't want the meeting to happen again in the near future.

9. If you want to restrict the meeting to a specific channel, click Add channel button to pick the channel you want to use. You might, for instance, wish to make it in a manager's channel to ensure only the team members subscribed to the channel are aware that there is a planned meeting.

10. The next field is the one where you add the location. In spite of its name "Location Selection," this does not actually involve choosing a physical location. It helps in selecting a room system enabled with Microsoft Teams and linked to the internet.

11. In the meeting field, located towards the bottom of your screen, enter the relevant information about the meeting.

12. When you are through, click the 'Send' button to add event to the calendar for MS Teams and invite the people added to the team.

5 COMMUNICATE VIA CHAT AND VIDEO CHAT OUTSIDE YOUR ORGANIZATION

5.1 Chatting With External Users and Guests

In a typical organization, an external user is a partner or a customer with whom you must communicate or collaborate. In Microsoft Teams, there are two types of external users: federated users and guests. The first category refers to users from another domain trusted by your organization. The second refers to users added as guests to your organization's Active Directory using their (personal or professional) e-mail addresses. You can chat with an external user or a guest like you chat with a colleague.

Your administrator must turn on external access, so you can call, chat, and schedule meetings with external (federated) users. Unlike guests, federated users do not have access to teams and channel resources and cannot be added to a group chat. For more details on what external and guest users can and cannot do, visit Microsoft's website at: https://docs.microsoft.com/en-us/microsoftteams/communicate-with-users-from-other-organizations.

6   THE BEST TEAMS APP

Apps in MS TEAMS are small applications or tools you use to do your job or complete a task. That is communicating and keeping in touch with your colleagues, teammates, or guests outside your organization – keep track of your work or tasks, add-ons to existing apps that add a new feature, and over-added value.

AttendanceBot is a Microsoft Teams App for managing staff timesheets, sick days, paid time off, and vacations. Its simple clock-in and clock-out messages allow you to keep track of employee time within Microsoft team meetings. It also exports timesheets, enabling you to monitor time spent on particular clients. You can then view the data on a dashboard.

6.1   Popular apps from third-party companies

If you're looking for ways to maximize your Teams productivity, you should consider downloading one of the many MS Teams apps. These tools allow you to organize and share your workspace with your entire team, and some of them are even free. Some of these applications are management-related, while others are simply for personal use. For instance, attendance bots like AttendanceBot let you track the hours that your team members work. They're easy to set up and require no technical knowledge.

Another great integration is with YouTube. You can search for and share videos using the Teams app. It's easy to create a playlist, add a link, and share the results. You can also pin the videos to your team channel tab for easy reference. These apps can even help you keep track of staff training videos. If you're looking for a new way to get the most out of your Microsoft Teams experience, consider one of these third-party apps.

Another useful tool is Remind. Remind allows you to set reminders from groups, channels, and personal messages. The interface is very easy to use, and you can set up recurring reminders and snooze alerts.

6.2 Freshdesk and Zendesk

Both Freshdesk (https://freshdesk.com/) and Zendesk (www.zendesk.com) have a variety of features and functions to improve customer service. They both have a comprehensive support page with a knowledge base, FAQ repository, and training videos. They both feature a quick-search bar, which is useful in locating specific information quickly. Freshdesk also lists an 800 number for last-minute support needs.

While both services offer basic ticket management features, Zendesk is more flexible with features such as view-based organization, custom conditions, filtering, and grouping tickets. Zendesk also offers pre-built dashboards that display business data in a clean and simple manner. In addition to ticket management, both services offer tools to manage people and collaborate in real-time.

Zendesk is more enterprise-friendly, however, and provides enterprise-grade support and a dedicated customer success team. However, it is important to note that both services have limited phone and live chat features.

Both have a Teams app that lets you get notified of the tickets delegated to you and your team.

6.3 Asana and Trello

Trello (https://trello.com/) and Asana (https://asana.com/) are the best Microsoft Teams apps to use when you need to collaborate on projects. They are easy to use and provide a great user experience. Users can create project templates and color-code tasks. Both tools help teams visualize project status and track progress.

Both Trello and Asana offer a free subscription. Trello is easier to use than Asana and is more visually oriented. Projects in Trello resemble a bulletin board with virtual cards that represent tasks. When a user clicks on a card, they can see information about the task, including the due date, checklist, and comments. Trello also allows you to drag and drop tasks and even customize the background to make them more personal.

Trello and Asana give team members a clear view of all project tasks. Teams can create all-team discussions and announcements and manage their projects in one place. Both apps make it easy to create and manage teams. Users can even create teams based on criteria, job roles, and more. Asana also allows you to collaborate with guest users and share your calendar.

6.4 Dropbox and Google Drive

Dropbox and Google Drive are both cloud storage services. Both of them offer similar functionality but differ in their user experience. Dropbox is more intuitive, and it has a desktop-like directory structure. You can access all your files from your desktop, and the file system is accessed quickly. Dropbox is a good option for people who work with large files, while Google is better for those who need access to documents from different locations.

Dropbox is a good choice for marketing workflows because it supports a variety of file types and features. For instance, Dropbox allows you to write content, review files, add comments, and deliver the final product to clients. It also allows you to easily store and share documents. It's also a good choice for content collaboration in Google Cloud, as it supports rich media and makes it easier to share content.

Dropbox is also great for collaboration, which is essential in today's remote-working world. If you need to access files from different locations, you can easily switch between desktop and mobile using your Dropbox account. Dropbox is also compatible with Microsoft Teams' mobile app, which allows you to collaborate with colleagues without leaving your office.

6.5 Twitter

You will keep up to date with Twitter (https:/twitter.com) without anyone ever leaving Teams when you enable the Microsoft Teams Twitter app. When you install the Twitter app, you'll get a channel connection to get tweets and follow hashtags on Twitter.

Another Twitter alternative is MailClark. This app acts as a shared inbox for messages sent to and from Microsoft Teams. This is useful for many different purposes, including customer support, marketing, recruitment, and sales. While Twitter is a popular social media site, it may not be the best choice for every company.

Adding Twitter to Microsoft Teams is easy. You can use the social networking site to share company updates and employee accomplishments. You can also add third-party Twitter apps to extend Microsoft Teams' features.

6.6 Salesforce

If you're looking for a way to seamlessly integrate Salesforce (www.salesforce.com) with Microsoft Teams, you've come to the right place.

Salesforce and Teams can be integrated to track and collaborate on opportunities. Opportunity feeds let team members view details of deals, players, and potential sales. Customer Support channels store contact information, and Salesforce integration allows team members to quickly collaborate with customers and respond to any issues. Similarly, Microsoft Teams and Salesforce can be integrated with a variety of other applications, including Microsoft Planner.

Microsoft and Salesforce both have loftier ambitions for their collaboration products. Both are trying to be the de facto collaboration platform for enterprises. However, each company has different goals for its customers. Salesforce has an enterprise-grade focus on quick messaging, while Microsoft focuses more on systems that can support the bulk of daily work. Application providers are also building productivity features into their own products, which challenges Salesforce's vision for the future of the collaboration market.

6.7 Kronos

Kronos (www.kronos.com) is a business collaboration software that helps organizations manage their team members. It provides real-time alerts, centralized policy management, and staffing forecasts through advanced optimization algorithms. It also includes self-service capabilities for employees, including instant access to project lists. This is a great choice for organizations of all sizes, including small and medium businesses.

The main feature of this Microsoft Teams app is that it is fully integrated with the Microsoft Teams platform. It helps teams keep track of upcoming meetings and allows participants to add notes, assign presenters, and set objectives. Users can also share agendas and vote, and the app syncs with Microsoft Planner. This makes it ideal for teams that meet on a regular basis.

Kronos has a variety of business-specific solutions for time and attendance management. It integrates with existing time clock systems, as well as mobile apps. It also offers a time-off management system and a physical time clock. Kronos' InTouch time-clocks feature a 7-inch touchscreen that allows employees to punch in and out with a swipe of their badge. Employees can also view their schedules and request time off, and review their work schedules.

6.8 GitHub

The GitHub app for Microsoft Teams recently entered the public preview phase. The app offers new features, including subscriptions and comment threading, that make it easier to collaborate on coding projects. According to the company's blog post, the app will help developers manage and coordinate coding projects without leaving Teams. It also includes a subscription feature, which lets you set notifications for pending pull requests, issues, and commits.

The GitHub app for Microsoft Teams connects with the two most important work spaces: GitHub and Microsoft Teams. This makes it easier to collaborate and monitor work. The app also includes a threading feature, which groups all pull requests and issues under a single primary card, displaying the latest status and meta-data. You can also create, close, and reopen issues with the GitHub app. It also sends push notifications to help you stay updated.

Another great feature of GitHub is its ability to connect with other apps. It is a popular source-code repository that gives developers access to tools to build better software. With GitHub and Microsoft Teams, developers can collaborate on code, chat, and share files easily. This means that they can get their work done more quickly and efficiently.

6.9 Connectors in TEAMS

Users use connectors to subscribe and receive messages and notifications from web services. Connectors automatically update the team with current content direct to a particular channel. Such updates can be from services like GitHub, Twitter, SharePoint, Azure, Trello, etc., in the conversation feed – in the post tab of a channel.

1. You Click the **ellipses** for "**More options**" on your chosen channel and Click the "Connectors" option from the pop-out menu.

2. You Click the "**Add**" button next to the connector you wish to add on the pop-up page starting with the title "Connectors for…".

3. You Click the "**Add**" button again on the pop-up page for that connector, for instance, the "**RSS**" connector, as illustrated below.

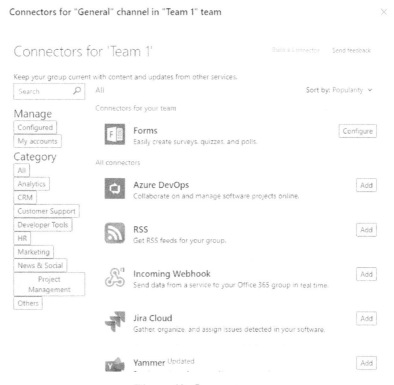

Figure 10: Connectors

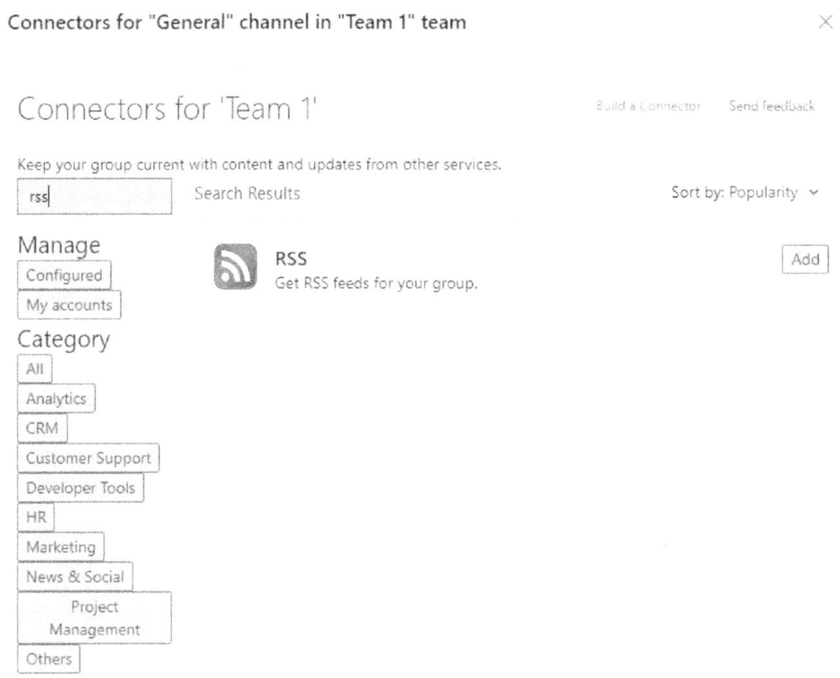

Connectors for "General" channel in "Team 1" team   ✕

Connectors for 'Team 1'   Build a Connector   Send feedback

Keep your group current with content and updates from other services.

rss   Search Results   Sort by: Popularity ∨

Manage   RSS   Add
Configured   Get RSS feeds for your group.
My accounts

Category
All
Analytics
CRM
Customer Support
Developer Tools
HR
Marketing
News & Social
Project
Management
Others

Figure 11: RSS Connector

There are many apps that you get notifications from in a channel. One such app is SharePoint News, as illustrated below in Figure 86. The news feature on your SharePoint site keeps your team engaged with important or interesting stories. When you add the **"SharePoint News"** App connector to your channel, a notification message is sent each time a new News post is published on your site.

> ***Note:*** *The **"SharePoint News"** App shows news from your SharePoint site in your conversation feeds in your channel's "Post" tab. You can configure an app after you have added it.*

When you create a connector for SharePoint News, the "SharePoint News" connector listens for any news published on the SharePoint team site for a given team. When there is new news content, this connector will publish a message in the "Post" feed to that news article in the connected channel.

7 TIPS, TRICKS & FAQ WITH COMMON PROBLEMS AND SOLUTIONS

Microsoft Teams have several skills, and using the tips and tricks provided in this section can enhance the use of Teams.

Stay in the Activity Warning Loop

The Activity tab will alert you when someone @mentions you, likes something you've written, or addresses a thread you've started. The Operation Bell number shows how many alerts you've been waiting for. The Activity tab is located at the top of the navigation panel on the left. So what's going on with your activity feed?

Using Immersive Reader to allow text to get narrated to you

One of Microsoft teams' most overlooked features; the immersive reader lets you read the text aloud at varying speeds. This function is useful when your eyeballs are busy elsewhere, but you still need to catch the textual details you get.

Click on the 3 dots on any message to start the immersive reader, and pick the reader from your drop-down menu.

Find Relevant Data By Cutting through Clutter With @Mentions

You can cut through the clutter and filter the content you see with @Mentions when a communication explosion occurs in various channels. It can differentiate your text and to-do lists from the other conversation

Visit a specific content Later by using the bookmark feature

Microsoft Teams allows you to bookmark certain content that you can later revisit. This way, when you need it, you will spend less time searching for essential data despite less relevant information.

Using slash commands to work quickly

Agile navigation is necessary if you want to get the job done quickly. Microsoft Teams allows this by giving you the option to use slash commands. For example, you can use /WhatsNew to test whether you have not missed out on something new. This command will carry you through the T-bot channel to the Release Notes Tab. Several of the slash commands most widely used in Microsoft Teams include:

- /Files – Latest files exchanged with you can be viewed
- /GoTo – you can enter a channel right away
- /call – launches a call with other leaders on the team
- /help – enables you to get help through T-bot
- /Saved- Directs you to your saved messages

Build a special working experience by using a Personalized View of Applications and Contacts

Each employee has a host of favorite apps to get the job done. In addition, you can build a special working environment just for you using Microsoft Teams.

You can see the tasks and things allocated to you from the planner, Jira cloud, etc., by accessing Personal App Space

Use the hide and show feature in teams to remain organized

Working through a sorted list of channels makes it easier to get the job done. Microsoft Teams let you pick the channels and teams you want to see and hide. Tap on the three dots next to a team or channel, and then press on more. Clicking on hiding will hide the team or channel.

Have company wikis in one location to boost collaboration

Wikis is an excellent feature inside Microsoft teams that enhances collaboration. In the left-hand menu, click on the three dots, and select the Wiki option. It will take you to the homepage of the Wiki, where you can take notes. You may also receive a list of all wikis about you by clicking on the All tab.

To translate non-English communication, use Inline Message Translation

This feature enables you to translate any message that you receive into any language other than English.

Grant access to people outside the company to communicate with others

When you want to communicate with a member outside your organization, you can use Microsoft teams to provide them with safe guest access. Guests are also permitted to attend meetings and view documents.

MS App Studio To Get Applications Made For Your Need

You can use MS App Studio to get unique applications that match your needs. It helps businesses to use Teams terminology to create their tools

Use bots for Microsoft teams to boost work by using some automation

MS teams have some pre-made bots for getting work done quickly. Some of the common ones are:

• Polly: this bot lets you keep track of employee engagement and poll members.

• WhoBot: this bot will let you know your colleagues.

• Grow bot: this bot lets you exchange kudos with members of the team

• Stats Bot: This bot delivers scheduled reports from outlets like Google Analytics.

Analyze Microsoft Team Usage By Members By Using Analytics and Reports

You can use the report feature to monitor how workers use Microsoft Teams. It will give you more visibility into the tool's most-used functionality and applications. By visiting the admin center of Teams, you will access files. Click Analytics and Reports button and choose the report to preview. In Teams, only the service admin can pull a report.

Record meetings for later access or share on all groups at a go

Microsoft Teams provides the option of recording meetings and screen sharing. The recorded meetings can be saved on Microsoft Stream. Recording can be done by clicking on the three dots in the channel and choosing Start Recording.

Prioritize shifts By using the shift function to control first-line staff

Shifts functionality helps managers to fix issues surrounding job shifts. With this function, they can schedule where a particular team's support is required in excess. You can access this function by clicking on the three dots and selecting Shifts.

Using Proximity Sensing to join A Meeting

This feature will detect Microsoft team room systems for the teams within your device's Bluetooth range. This way, you'd be able to find a place to get on a meeting collaboration easily. You can do this by going through available room systems near you after launching the team meeting.

8 ADMINISTRATOR TEAMS

If you are your organization's admin, you might be required to help your organization set up the Teams interface. Setting up the Teams interface might entail assigning moderators to channels, updating the teams for more effective collaboration, and assigning team owners to teams that don't have owners. The MS Teams admin center allows you to manage the team in your organization and control all that is happening within the team just by clicking or tapping some essential features. As an admin, you can check admin center through https://admin.microsoft.com. Only the Global administrator or the Teams service administrator can access the admin center to use most of the available tools.

The organization's admin can manage meeting settings from the MS Teams admin center by going to *Meetings* and tapping on *Meeting settings*.

✓ **Allow anonymous users to join the meeting:** When the anonymous join is enabled, anybody can join team meeting as anonymous member by using the link present in meeting invitation. The admin can allow anonymous join using the Microsoft admin center by following these steps;

- Visit the admin center, which is accessible at https://admin.teams. microsoft.com.

- From admin center's left navigation pane, visit **Meetings,** and tap on **Meeting settings.**

- Scroll to **Participants,** and toggle ON the *anonymous can join* header.

- You can toggle off the settings if you don't want an anonymous identity to enter your meeting.

✓ **Customizing meeting invitations:** You can add any other information when sending a meeting invitation. Your organization can add its logo, other websites, or product links to the invite sent out. To customize your meeting invitation, follow these tips

- Visit the admin center, which is accessible at https://admin.teams. microsoft.com.

- In the admin center on the left navigation pane, visit **Meetings,** and tap on **Meeting settings.**

- Scroll to the **E-mail invitation,** and carry out the following actions;

  - **Logo URL:** You can type the address where you save the organization's logo.

  - **Legal URL:** Fill in the URL if the company has a website people can visit for any issue relating to legal concerns.

  - **Help URL:** People can visit this link for help with any issues.

  - **Footer:** Enter a footer message.

- Tap **Save** to finish.

- Wait for some time for these settings to take effect. Then you can try to send out an invite to preview what the meeting invite will look like.

Team overview grid

To access all the management tools for Teams, the administrator should swipe to the Team node in the admin center by selecting *Teams* and then tap on *manage Teams.* The Microsoft grid has the following features embedded;

- **Team identity:** This is usually the team's name designated by the admin.

- **Channels:** This shows you the number of channels that have been created.

- **Team members:** This displays the total number of members in the team.

- **Owners:** The total number of teams' owners in the team. Team owners can be more than two.

- **Guests:** Indicates the number of guest users in the team.

- **Privacy:** Shows the kind of access type the backing Microsoft 365 group has.

- **Status:** Shows either archived or active condition of the team.

- **Description:** This tells you information about the Microsoft 365 plan from which the particular Microsoft Teams you are using has been unboxed.

- **Classification:** This tells you information about the classification of the Microsoft 365 plan from which the particular Microsoft Teams you are using has been unboxed.

- **Group ID:** This shows the distinctive Group ID of the Microsoft 365 plan from which the particular Microsoft Teams you are using has been unboxed.

- **Note:** Sometimes, you might not see all of these features in the admin center grid, but you can tap the *"edit column icon* and then toggles on/off any feature you want to add from the column. Tap *"Apply"* when you are done to effect the change.

Adding a new Team

- Select *"Add"* when you need to add a new team. The *"Add a new team"* page will be prompted, where you can assign names and descriptions to the team. Set the group to private or public, depending on what you want. Also, set the team's classification.

Editing the team

- To edit any group and carry out some team-designated settings, tap any team you want to edit and select edit by the left of the team's name.

Archiving a team

- The admin can archive the team by setting the team into a read-only mode.

Deleting a team

- Once you delete the entire Microsoft 365 package, Microsoft Teams will be deleted. A deleted team can be restored because it is only soft-deleted for 30 days before you can no longer have access to it. For example, you can restore a deleted account as an admin by navigating to the admin center. Tap the *"expand groups icon"* and select *"Deleted groups."* Choose the group you wish to restore, and then tap **Restore groups.**

Searching the Teams

· You can search the team name field by deploying the string *"Begins with"*

Making adjustments to Teams

· Right from team profile page, you can have access to change any of the following features or settings;

· **Members:** the admin can add or remove any member he wishes, even promote a group member as owner, or stripe a group owner with his permission.

· **Channels:** The Admin can create a new channel and remove or edit any previously created channel. The default general channel cannot be deleted.

· **Team name:** The Admin can alter the team name to edit it or give it another name entirely.

· **Team description:** The Admin can alter the team description to edit it or write another description for the team entirely.

· **Privacy:** The Admin can decide whether the team should be private or accessible to everyone.

· **Classification:** The Admin can choose any of the three classifications, which include; Confidential, highly confidential, and general.

· **Conversations settings:** The Admin can decide whether to allow members to edit and delete messages from the group.

· **Channel settings:** the admin can decide whether to allow group members to create a new channel or edit a previously created channel.

Troubleshooting Teams

- Sometimes, minor errors can occur during the process of operating Teams. These minor errors can be corrected by changing some of the settings within the Microsoft 365 groups or the Team interface. Check the following troubleshooting strategies;

- Team members missing from the grid: This can be caused by incorrect team profiling by the system. This can lead to a missing property before the system can recognize the team. You can solve this by setting the missing property to the actual value using MS Graph.

From The Admin's Perspective

For this, you need to enter the Microsoft 365 admin center and go down into Microsoft Teams.

Before you go there, flip over to "**Teams & groups,**" then "**Active teams & groups,**" and locate the team you just created.

You can see that it's created a Microsoft 365 group for that team. If you click on the group here, which is quite essential that you do, and click on "**Members,**" it shows you all the members, but if you go into "**Settings,**" this is important; if you want the team to be contactable externally, then allow external senders to e-mail this group, send copies of group e-mails, and you can change the privacy here as well.

Now the one thing that you cannot change is once it becomes a team, that's it. Essentially a team is an extended Microsoft 365 group. It is extended because you can use third-party products here as well.

Administering the team templates

In your admin center, you're going to click on the drop-down arrow for Teams, and here, you're going to come into "**Teams templates.**" Here is a complete list, and this is useful because you get a description of exactly what the team is. You can see who published the team template (now there are hundreds of templates out there, and several third-party providers are also providing these templates). It shows you how many channels, how many apps the team had, and when it was last modified. So, you can see that you've got the same templates here, and you may be wondering if it is easy to create a template here. Click on the "**Add**" button, and just as you saw in Microsoft Teams, you can create a new template, use an existing template or start with an existing template.

You can go ahead and create a new template. Give it a name, put a little description in here, and you can specify the locale; if your demo tenant is in the US, you would need to use a US-based tenant. Click on "**Next**" to proceed. Note that if you try and click on next and don't have a description, you need to go ahead and put that in before proceeding.

Now, you're going to enter how many channels you want. So, you'll click on "**Add**" and enter the channel(s) details. Then, you're just going to apply that and add that channel to the template.

You can also add apps as well if you want to. So, you can bring in an app by simply typing the app's name. Any app that's grayed out shows me that the app is already in there, so you get that by default, but if there are any third-party ones, then, of course, you would go ahead and add those.

So, go ahead, click on "Submit," and see that you've created this template. Any templates you create will go straight to the top of the list, which is very similar to other Microsoft products.

So that's typically how you create the templates. If you go back to one of the other templates here, you can see that this tells you a little bit about the template; you've got an excellent description here, the number of channels and apps, and each template has its unique ID here. It shows me which channels have got which apps applied to them, so some planning is often helpful here. Finally, you can go into the apps; it shows you which apps are here, and you can click on them to get more details.

Next in your journey of administering templates is called "**Template policies**." Again, there is a global policy that contains pretty much all the templates, but you might want to create your template policy and then assign that policy along with those templates to your users.

What you can do is go ahead and add a Template policy. Then, you can decide which templates you want to show and hide. Notice that you're not deleting the template; all you're doing is you're just hiding that specific template here. Again, you can put in a description, and once you've done that, you can scroll down and see that it gives you a list of those hidden templates. So, you click on "**Save,**" and now that this is selected, you can decide if you want to assign this template to any particular user.

When you search for names in teams, you need to search for a minimum of three characters. This is because when the users log into teams, these templates will be the only two templates they see, and it shows you which templates have been distributed and how many users have been applied there.

The other thing we have here is "**Teams update policies,**" If you go into the default settings here, this means how often you want Teams to be updated. This used to be in organizational-wide settings, but it's worth mentioning here because if you enable the "**Office preview,**" you'll get new features updated, including Teams templates.

9 THE STRATEGIC SHORTCUTS

Save time with keyboard shortcuts

Using keyboard shortcuts can be faster than using a mouse or touch screen and is especially useful for disabled users. The list is broken down by category, including General, Guide, Messages, Meetings, and Calls, so users can easily find the shortcuts they need.

General

Function	In Desktop application
Display keyboard shortcuts	Ctrl + (.) period
Display commands	Ctrl + (/) slash
Initiate a chat	Ctrl + N
Access a specific channel or team	Ctrl + G
Open **Search**	Ctrl + E
Access filter	Ctrl + Shift + F
Access settings	Ctrl + (,) comma
Access apps flyout	Ctrl + (') accent
Zoom out (Enlarge)	Ctrl + (-) Minus
Zoom in (Diminish)	Ctrl + (=) Equals
Reset zoom to default	Ctrl + (0) Zero
Access help	F1
Close	Esc (Escape)

Messaging

Function	In desktop application
Initiate a conversation	Ctrl + N
Access compose box	Alt (left) + Shift + C
Enlarge compose box	Ctrl + Shift + X
Go to new line	Shift + Enter

Function	In desktop application
Send message	Ctrl + Enter
Search current channel or chat messages	Ctrl + F
Reply to a thread	Alt (left) + Shift + R
Mark important message	Ctrl + Shift + I

Navigation

Function	In Desktop application
Access **calendar**	Ctrl + 4
Access **Files**	Ctrl + 6
Access **Chats**	Ctrl + 2
Access **Calls**	Ctrl +5
Access **Teams**	Ctrl +3
Access **Activity**	Ctrl + 1
Shift selected team up	Ctrl + Shift + Up arrow
Shift selected team down	Ctrl + Shift + Down arrow
Access previous list item	Alt (left) + Up arrow
Access next list item	Alt (left)+ Down arrow
Return to previous section	Ctrl+Shift+F6
Proceed to next section	Ctrl+F6
Access the **History** menu	Ctrl + Shift + H
Get an open app	Ctrl + F6

Calls and Meetings

Function	In desktop application
Initiate audio call	Ctrl + Shift + C
Initiate video call	Ctrl + Shift + U
Receive audio call	Ctrl + Shift + S

Function	In desktop application
Receive video call	Ctrl + Shift + A
Dismiss audio call	Ctrl + Shift + H
Dismiss video call	Ctrl + Shift + H
Refuse call	Ctrl + Shift + D
Raise your hand	Ctrl + Shift + K
Lower your hand	Ctrl + Shift + K
Call out raised hand	Ctrl + Shift + L
Mute	Ctrl + Shift + M
Unmute	Ctrl + Spacebar
Toggle video	Ctrl + Shift + O
Initiate screen share session	Ctrl + Shift + E
Access sharing toolbar	Shortcut not available
Admit screen share	Ctrl + Shift + A
Refuse screen share	Ctrl + Shift + D
Screen Current list	Ctrl + Shift + F
Access **Background settings** menu	Ctrl + Shift + P
Let in people from lobby announcement	Ctrl + Shift + Y
Send or Save meeting request	Ctrl + S
Check day	Ctrl + Alt (left) + 1
Check week	Ctrl + Alt (left) + 3
Check work week	Ctrl + Alt (left) + 2
Proceed to next day or week	Ctrl + Alt(left)+Right arrow
Return to previous day or week	Ctrl + Alt(left) +Left arrow
Access current time	Alt (left) + (.) period
Schedule meeting	Alt (left) + Shift + N
Join through meeting details	Alt(left) + Shift + J
Move to suggested time	Alt(left) + Shift + S

10 CONCLUSION

Microsoft Teams is an excellent option for businesses of all sizes and can help enhance employee collaboration. While adding Microsoft Teams may be more time consuming than other functionalities in Office 365, the added functionality it enables can be worth it. It can be an effective way for businesses to communicate. It also provides a more streamlined experience when communicating with customers, reducing the number of communications that need to be handled. As a business grows and the number of employees and customers increases, it becomes increasingly difficult to manage communications on multiple channels. Using Microsoft Teams, you can easily enable commercial communications while standardizing your messaging protocol.

Printed in Great Britain
by Amazon

19218588R00027